GREETINGS!
From a Distance

By Dr Zewlan Moor
Illustrated by Romulo Reyes III

Library For All Ltd.

LIBRARY FOR ALL

DIGITAL EDUCATION · FOR THE WORLD

Library For All is an Australian not for profit organisation with a mission to make knowledge accessible to all via an innovative digital library solution. Visit us at libraryforall.org

Greetings! From a Distance

First published 2022

Published by Library For All Ltd
Email: info@libraryforall.org
URL: libraryforall.org

This book was made possible by the generous support of the June Canavan Foundation.

Original illustrations by Romulo Reyes III

Greetings! From a Distance
Dr Moor, Zewlan
ISBN: 978-1-922827-26-5
SKU04095

GREETINGS!
From a Distance

If you cannot shake hands or hug, how can you greet your friends?

You can say, "Hello!" That works. Unless your friend is hard of hearing.

Or a long way away.
Then you can shout.
Or speak into a
megaphone.

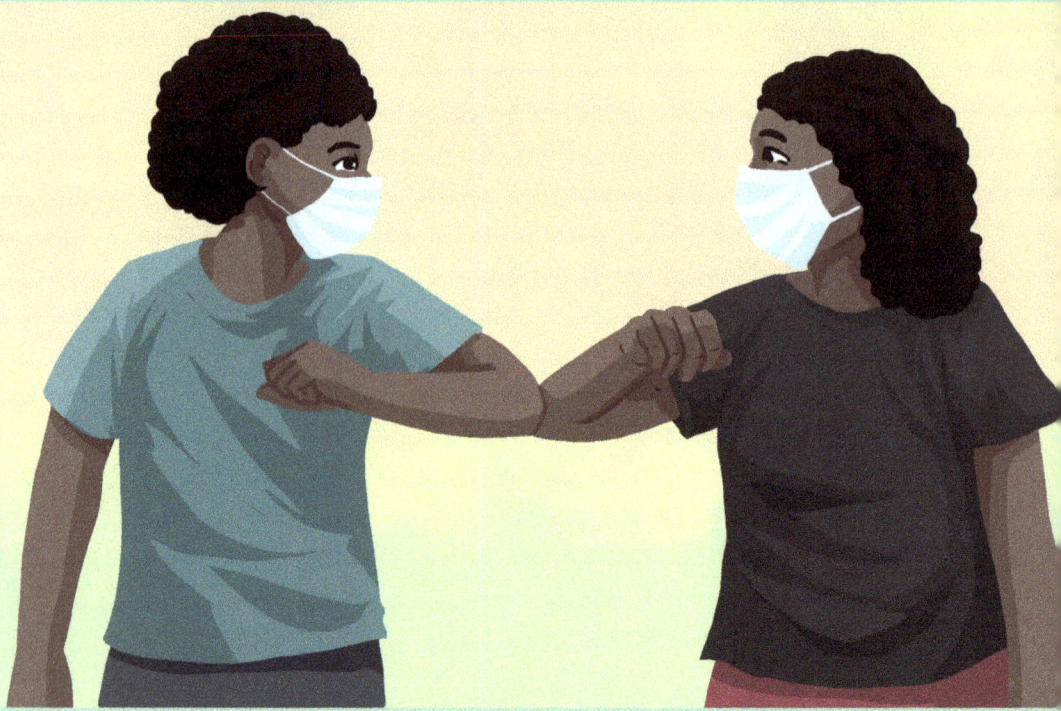

You can elbow tap.
Or foot tap.
That would keep your
hands clean.
This works! But you
would not be socially
distanced.
You would still be
breathing on each other!

Do you have any other ideas for how to greet your friends when you are more than 1 metre apart?
Can you copy the greetings of other living things?

Why not meet and greet like a fish?

Glub-glub-glub.
Can you make a fish face?
Your friend might think you are blowing them a kiss!

Meet and greet like a chicken.

Scratch-scratch-scratch.
This is a good one if you
have lost something. You can
scratch around on the ground
with your feet while you look
for it. But your friend might
think you are rude.

Meet and greet like a tree
kangaroo.
Squint your eyes and look all
shy and cute.

Meet and greet like a singing dog.

Aaarooooo!
Wolf howl meets whale song. This is the perfect greeting for long distances.

Meet and greet like a pig.

Snuffle-oink! Snuffle-oink!
Hmmm. This greeting might not be very polite. Your friend might think you are thinking of your next meal more than you are thinking of them.

Meet and greet like a crocodile.

Snap-snap-snap.
Stop! Don't do this one.
It is not very friendly.

Maybe you should stick with human greetings.

Can you think of other ways you can greet your friends?

You can wave.

You can wink.

You can bow.

You can pull a funny face.

17

You can smile. Just not like a crocodile.

But what if you are wearing a mask?

If you cannot show your mouth or teeth, make sure your smile reaches your eyes. Plump up those cheeks. Make your eyes crinkle. And shine. And sparkle.

You can make signs with words and drawings. Put them up where your friends will see them. It might cheer up their day.

There are lots of ways to meet and greet your friends! You can stay connected, even while social distancing.

SOME PUZZLING QUESTIONS:

Why does everyone keep talking about social distancing?

When people are sick with an infectious lung disease, they can pass it on to others through respiratory droplets when they are sick, and even a few days before. Respiratory droplets are small droplets of particles, including cells, saliva and mucus from the airway, as well as infections in the form of viruses and bacteria. These droplets are heavy and are expelled when we breathe and talk. They are transmitted even further when we cough or sneeze.

If we stay 1 metre away from everyone, we have the best chance of not getting infected through being exposed to respiratory droplets. And then the virus will die out, because it needs humans to live in. Our best chance of getting rid of the COVID-19 virus is to stay 1 metre away from people outside our social "bubble".

What is a social bubble?

This is the group of people you hang out with most of the time. It might be your family. Or family friends you live with. It might be other children at your school or residence.

It might be a few people. Or a large number of family members living in one household. The main thing is that this is the group you do things with. If you go for a walk to the shops or market with people in your bubble, you have to make sure you stay 1 metre away from all other people.

Those people might be by themselves, or in their own bubble. If one person in your bubble gets infected, they might end up passing it onto other people in your bubble. But the spread will be limited to your bubble only, if you are staying away from everyone else.

23

SOME MORE PUZZLING QUESTIONS:

Why should we not shake hands?
Not shaking hands stops the transfer of disease. Viruses, such as COVID-19, and bacteria, such as shigella, are passed on to other people via our hands. Either by touching hands directly, or by touching things the other person has touched.

Why should we not hug?
Respiratory droplets can rest on our clothes and other people can pick them up onto their clothes and hands if they hug us. Then, if they touch their mouth and especially their eyes, the virus can enter the body. If they touch the nose, the virus will likely set up camp in the moist, warm environment and land on snot and other nasal secretions, which can then be passed on accidentally by touching or picking your nose, or by sneezing.

Why should we cough into our elbow?
Remember we said respiratory droplets spray out the most when you cough? It's best to limit their spread by coughing into your elbow. Not your hand, because then you will pass the droplets on to everything you touch.

25

You can use these questions to talk about this book with your family, friends and teachers.

What did you learn from this book?

Describe this book in one word. Funny? Scary? Colourful? Interesting?

How did this book make you feel when you finished reading it?

What was your favourite part of this book?

download our reader app
getlibraryforall.org

About the author

Dr Zewlan (pronounced "Shoolen") Moor is an Australian medical doctor and author whose passion for social justice was formed on childhood visits to family in the Philippines. The stark inequalities she saw at the age of 8 made a lasting impression. She is thrilled to be published by a publisher who embraces the United Nations Sustainable Development Goals—Library For All. It fulfils two long-held dreams: to contribute to international public health through health promotion; and to bring the joy of reading and language to all children.

Did you enjoy this book?

We have hundreds more expertly curated original stories to choose from.

We work in partnership with authors, educators, cultural advisors, governments and NGOs to bring the joy of reading to children everywhere.

Did you know?

We create global impact in these fields by embracing the United Nations Sustainable Development Goals.

libraryforall.org

www.ingramcontent.com/pod-product-compliance
Lightning Source LLC
Chambersburg PA
CBHW040315050426
42452CB00018B/2851